Spear Masters

Comprehension Book 1

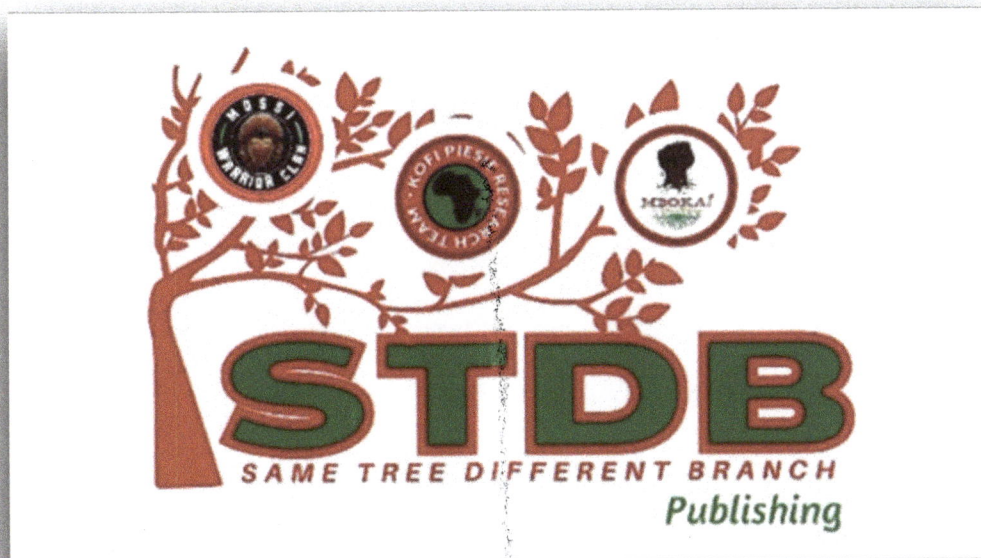

SameTreeDifferent Branch Publishing

Same Tree Different Branch Publishing

Copyright 2021by Kofi Piesie Research Team

Printed in the United States of America

SPEAR

MASTERS

INSTITUTION

This image is of a boy from the Dinka tribe who holds his spear at a cattle camp in Mingkaman. During South Sudan's dry season between December and May, pastoralists from the highlands move to the lowlands and close to the Nile, where they set up big cattle camps to make sure their animals are close to grazing land. These young men tend to the cattle and protect their cattle from wild animals and perpetrators trying to steal their cattle. If you want to know more about the Dinka Tribes that live in South Sudan, get our scholarly book Spear Masters: A Historical Survey in The Minds Of African Warrior Scholars Vol. 4.

WELCOME

Chavis Tp hsb McCray

On the behalf of the Kofi Piesie Research Team, I would like to welcome the reader and future warrior scholar to the Spear Masters Institution Comprehension Book One. This is an ingenious and innovative solution straight out the immaculately creative mind of Kofi Piesie himself to focus on perfecting our youth's ability to comprehend via the sharpening of critical thinking skills with this workbook full of reading exercises and powerful information brought directly to the reader from individuals dedicated to the assistance of advancing our youth's intellectual capabilities via the use of historical, cultural, and informational literacy as the catalyst for the development of the minds of future New Independent Afrikan Academy warrior scholars. The authors made every attempt at making sure the information provided in this publication is accurate and well researched to the best of their ability. We are the embodiment of Kofi Piesie motto and title of his first solo publication, "As I learn, We all learn," which if you don't have by now, we encourage you to at some point acquire (along with the rest of our large body of work) to add to the larger scope of reader's edification process. Jama (PEACE) Mboka (FAMILY)

Lesson 1

"Spear Master"

Kofi Piesie

The Dinka says, according to their folktale, that long ago, there were dances held by lions, and a man was dancing when a lion looked at him and demanded his bracelet. The man refused to give his bracelet to the lion, after which the lion bit his thumb entirely off. Then the man bled to death. The man had left a wife and daughter behind, but they had no son, and so the widow went weeping to the river. The river spirit heard her and asked her what was wrong. When she told the story of her misfortune, the river spirit said to her, "Lift your skirt and brush the waves toward you so that they enter your body."

The spirit gave her a spear and told her that the spear was a symbol of her bearing a male child. He also gave her a fish for food and told her to go home and relax without delay. The woman went home and soon bore a son, Aiwel, who had a complete set of teeth when he was born, a sign of unusual spiritual powers.

As an infant, he was left sleeping on the floor, but when the mother came back into the room, she noticed that a gourd of milk had been drunk. Not believing that it could have been the infant, she accused her daughter of stealing the milk. She punished the daughter. The same thing happened over and over again. The mother was quite disturbed by this situation and soon became suspicious. She acted like she was leaving the baby alone with the milk, but she thought she should hide in the bushes and watch the baby as she went out. She did this and, to her surprise, saw the baby Aiwel get up from the floor and drink the milk. She opened the door and accused him of drinking the milk. He told her not to tell anybody, or she would die. She could not keep the secret to herself, and she died as Aiwel had said. He had begun to develop the power of the Spear Masters to make his words come true.

He could no longer live with his mother's death. He went to stay with the spirit father in the river until he grew up. He left the river as a man with an ox of many colors, representing all colors of his cattle. The ox was named Longar, and from then on, the man was Aiwel's Longar. Aiwel then decided to tell the village elders that they had to leave that place to avoid the death of all their cattle. He went and said to them that he would show them where there was a big pasture and no death.

They refused to believe him. So, he went by himself and found the place, and his cattle prospered. But soon the people tried to follow him, but it was more difficult now. At one river they were trying to cross, Aiwel stood on the other side of the river, encouraging them, but he would kill them with his spear as they came up out of the reeds.

Then one of the men, Agothyathik, saw what was happening and decided to play a trick on Aiwel. He would take a large ox bone and give it to a friend to take across the river, holding it on a pole in front of him as he crossed. When Aiwel saw this, he thought it was a human and tried to spear it. Just then, Agothyathik grabbed him and wrestled him to the ground.

Finally, Aiwel tired and gave up the wrestling and told Agothyathik to bring the people over. Some were afraid, but to those who came, Aiwel gave fishing spears to carry when they prayed and war spears when they fought. He gave them deities to worship and a blue bull whose thighbone would be sacred to them. The men who received the spears became leaders of clans that are spear masters who keep the most perfect way. In the end, the Spear Masters were those who followed the straight path, walked erect, and taught others the lessons of Aiwel that the spear could be used for good, as in fishing, or for defending the clan against enemies as in warfare.

Aiwel Longar represents so many values, attitudes, and dispositions in Dinka philosophy that one could almost say that the Dinka measure other humans by the characteristics of Aiwel Longar. First of all, his narrative is epic and shows that he had arisen from a unique condition of being from the spiritual and the human side. Second, he overcame all conditions of difference and established himself as the leader of his people.

Now the Spear Masters are those who learned lessons of good and evil as represented in the use of the spear. Those who contribute to this comprehension book I deem modern Spear Masters that has learned lessons of good and evil, as illustrated in the use of the pen. The pen, just like the spear, can be used for good or evil, but we use our pen/spear to fight against pseudoisms, misinformation that might hurt and harm our people. We also use the spear/pen in this publication "Spear Masters Institution Comprehension book 1, to help our young teenagers raise their comprehension level.

Questions

1). After the water spirit gave the women a spear, the spear symbolized what?

2). The woman went home and soon bore a son name what?

3). The woman caught her baby on the floor drinking what?

4). After Aiwel mother's death, who did he go live with?

5). Did the village elders listen to Aiwel after he told them that they had to leave that place to avoid the death of all their cattle?

6). After Aiwel got tired and gave up the wrestling and told Agothyathik to bring the people over the river, what two spears he gave them when they prayed and fought?

7). The men who received the spears became leaders of the clans that were called what?

8). For the Dinka, the spear could be used for what?

9). The Spear Masters were those who followed?

10). To the Dinka Aiwel represent what?

Lesson 2

1811 AMERICA'S LARGEST REVOLT

By Brother Lavelle

For us to study American History, we have to bring up the impact that Louisiana has. This revolt was inspired by the Haitian Revolution, and it became the largest uprising in American History.

Jan. 8-10, 1811 African slaves set off an uprising in St. John The Baptist Parish on the east bank of the Mississippi River. Which is today Laplace, Louisiana, nearby the city of New Orleans. (The Territory of Orleans is on the German coast)

Charles Deslondes was a leader of this revolt, assembling the slaves from plantation to plantation. Gathering anywhere from between 200 to 500 men, they marched for 20 miles and 2 days, burning down plantations, sugar houses, and crops.

White men formed a coalition to stop this insurrection of these men with hand tools. January 10, the White militia assassinated 45 evaded slaves while no harm was done on the other side.

Weeks later, the militia tracked down the other slaves, interrogated and lynched them. They placed their heads on pikes to frighten the other slaves so that another revolt like this would never happen.

The militia executed 95 slaves and viciously slew Charles Deslondes. Only two of the members of the white militia died during this American Revolt.

KEY DEFINITIONS

•Revolt: 1. To renounce allegiance or subjection (as to a government) Rebel. 2: to experience disgust or shock. To turn away with disgust.

•Insurrection: an act or instance of revolting against civil authority or an established government.

•Militia: a part of the organized armed forces of a country liable to call only in an emergency.

(Keyword definitions were used from MERRIAM WEBSTER DICTIONARY)

Questions

1). Where did the revolt take place?

2). Define **revolt**?

3). Define insurrection?

4). What chronological event inspired this uprising?

5). How many days did this last?

6). Why did the white militia put the slave's heads on Pikes?

7). How many slaves died in this?

8). True or False. Was Nat Turner the leader in this rebellion?

9). What's the total of the white militia that died?

10). Provide the meaning of **militia?**

11). True or False. This rebellion underwent 5 days?

12). How many slaves assembled during the march?

13). True or False. Is New Orleans a city in Louisiana?

14). How lengthy were the miles they marched?

15). True or False. Does the Mississippi River run into Louisiana?

Lesson 3

A Concise Ornithological Primer:
Species Evolution and Eye Anatomy of Tyto alba

Djedemankh Heka Re

The Institute of Kemetic Philology

Rkhty Amen, founder

The barn owl (Tyto alba) is a member of one of only two known families of owls (Tytonidae, the other is Strigidae, known as the "true owl" family more commonly, both of the Strigiformes order). Found on every continent with the exception of Antarctica, it has a worldwide distribution and are mainstay in areas where humans live. We are going to take a closer look at the owl family evolution, as well as the barn owl's unique skull and eye features.

Barn owls, like all Aves (birds), evolved from dinosaurs (clade Dinosauria). The earliest ancestor we have for birds is Dromaeosaurus (Dromaeosaurus albertensis), of clade Theropoda, that lived during the Jurassic Period (around 160 MYA). This initial evolution took place over tens of millions of years and ended in the Cretaceous Period with a mass extinction event (Brusatte, et. al 2015). Aves are in the taxonomic clade Theropoda, but are even further narrowed down into another clade (Avialae) consisting of living dinosaurs (Senter 2007). For owls, in particular, the earliest ancestor lived during the Eocene Period (45 MYA), but the most recent ancestor for Tyto is found in the Middle Miocene (12 MYA). A now-extinct species appeared 8 MYA and gave rise to the modern T. alba during the Pleistocene (2.6 MYA).

The skull of T. alba averages around 69 mm (2.7 in) long, 40 mm (1.57 in) wide and 29 mm (1 in) tall. The defining feature of an owl skull is the sclerotic rings found on each ocular socket. These rings hold the eyes of the barn owl in place; unlike other birds, owls do not have eyeballs. The sclerotic rings hold the elongated retinae, which are in a front-to-back position, in place. There are no muscles in the corners to allow eye rotation. Peripheral eyesight is limited to about 110° (compared with 170° for humans), so owls must turn their whole head to see in any direction but forward. There is binocular overlap in their frontal vision due to a front-faced orientation of the eyes (Harmening & Wagner, 2011). Along with the Pharaoh Eagle Owl (Bubo ascalaphus), T. alba is featured most often in sS md.w nTr (Sesh Medu

Netcher, misnomered as Egyptian Hieroglyphics) as the symbol for the phonetic value /m/. The owl is the only bird featured in the script with the face, not in profile; the distinguishable features of both owl species are obstructed from a side view, partly due to the aforementioned optical configuration.

Questions

1). What are the two (2) clades barn owls (T. alba) are classified in?

2). How many owl families are there?

3). Do owls have eyeballs? Answer with either Yes or No.

4). What are the names of the owl families?

5). Name the skull feature that holds the eyes of owls in place.

6). What is the animal group that birds evolved from?

7). Name the six (6) continents the barn owl is found on.

8). What is the measurement for the peripheral vision of T. alba, in degrees?

9). What time period does Dromaeosaurus come from?

10). How long ago did the modern barn owl first appear?

11). In what period did the event that triggered the mass extinction of the dinosaurs occur?

12). What is the phonetic value represented by Strigiformes in Sesh Medu Netcher?

13). In what period did the evolution of birds from Dromaeosaurus occur?

14). How wide is the skull of a barn owl (in both mm and in)?

15). What taxonomic clade do modern birds share with Dromaeosaurus?

Lesson 4

A Mijikenda Warrior who fought the British one of Kenya's brave woman

(Mekatilili Wa Menza).

Okatakyie Kwabena Selikem Wiredu

Mekatilili Wa Menza was born around 1860 at Present-day Mutsara wa Tsatsu in Kilifi county in Present-day Kenya. She was a native Mijikenda, and she belonged to the Giriama, which is the sub-group of the Mijikenda ethnic group. Mekatilili was the only daughter of five siblings. One of her brothers, Mwarandu, was captured by Arab Slave masters and It is claimed Mwarandu was captured to what is now Present-day Pakistan from Kenya, and others claimed he was captured from Present-day Kenya to Present-day India. Mekatilili was 53 years old when British colonization began in Kenya.

The British was successful in establishing a number of rubber plantations in the Giriama area. Metatili Wa Menza was a very brave and brilliant woman who spoke harsh and threatened British Colonialism in 1913. She held a meeting, and it was organized by her and Giriama people which they planned to rebel against British Colonial government. Later she was described by the British as a devil who made herself a Prophetess, and She was never made herself a Prophetess, and she was not a devil. British wanted to tarnish her image, but the British feared her, so they spread Catholicism and their other religions in Violence.

It is believed Mekatilili escaped and crossed the north to Somalian border, then walked her entire way back to her home. She led Giriama resistance and moved towards open revolt with resources stretched thin due to World War I; the British ceased colonization efforts in the region.

According to African Researcher Kwabena Wiredu Selikem Okatakyie's account, Mekatilili Wa Menza was considered to have the same bravery being compared to Jamaica's Queen Nanny and Ghana's Yaa Asantewaa. She led her people, which is Giriama in a rebellion against British colonial administration and policies actively in 1913- 1914. Giriama are part of the Mijikenda subgroup who Inhabited the Kenyan coast; they had a sacred dwelling places known as Kaya, located in a forested area, one of which the British Colonial administration destroyed by dynamiting 1914.

According to Dr. Mussah Chekai account, The destroying as Kaya Fungo in 1914 Mekatilili, the Mijikenda Warrior, witnessed her brother being captured and enslaved by Arabs, followed by the British oppressing her people and white supremacy Violence. Mekatili fought tirelessly but was captured by the British and was exiled to Mumias. Mekatili never gave up but provoked the British and escaped from exile, then returned back home again. Mekatili Wa Menza finally declared war and was engaged in a cultural dance known as Kifudu.

She was one of the first Kenyan women to rise up against the British, and She took oaths and gave offerings to her Ancestors to restore their sovereignty. The Rebellion lasted from 1913 to 1914 between British and Giriama, and It is believed some Mijikenda warriors died before she died around the age of 70 in 1925.

Questions

1). Mekatilili Wa Menza was born where?

2). True or False Did Mekatilili have five brothers?

3). True or False Did the British establish a number of sugar plantations in the area of Giriama ?

4). True or False Did Mekatilili herself a prophetess?

5). Who Bravery was Mekatilili compared to?

6). The Giriama people are subgroup to who?

7). The sacred dwelling places known as Kaya was destroyed how?

8). Mekatilili was first Kenya women to do what?

9). Mekatilili took an oath and gave what to her Ancestors?

10). True or False did the rebellion last from 1913 to 1914 between the British and Giriama?

Lesson 5

African drums refresher course: Djembe Edition

Tchalla Bangoura

We should also be familiar with this topic if you've been keeping up with us over at Kofi Piesie Tv. We would like to thank each one of you for your loyalty and support. Without you, our words fall on deaf ears. Now on to the lesson, the importance of song, music, and dance in Africa is something that cannot be stressed enough. Especially when it comes to West African cultures, the **Malinke** have a rich tradition of all three, and it shines brightly through the light of **Djembe**. The origins of this goblet-shaped hand drum date back to roughly a thousand years ago, a time before this part of West Africa would be colonized by the French, and yet still, a long time after the Arab invasion. Fashioned out of beautiful mother nature, the blacksmiths of the community, the **Numu** would carve a beautiful instrument that has brought joy around the world since. Malinke **Griots** says that the village's women would sing and clap rhythms while they worked. Some of the Numu would go on to ask the ancestors for permission to "borrow" a piece of nature and transform a tree into a communication device that can be heard between villages. Once permission is granted, we have the birth of Djembe. This drum is hollowed out and has a skin on one side. Goatskin is traditionally used, but in some regions like the Ivory Coast and Burkina Faso, they sometimes use calf skin. The use of gazelle predates all other skin options as it was the first that was used to make the first Djembes. Those who play Djembe are named **Djembefola,** which is Malinke for "one who gives the Djembe voice."

We **NEVER PLAY DJEMBE WITH STICKS**. To properly give this drum its voice, one would play three basic sounds. They are bass (played in the center of the drum with the entire hand), tone (played at the edge of the drum with closed fingers), and slap (also played at the edge of the drum except with slightly open fingers). This will allow you to properly give the designated signals to orchestrate the dance with the music. Djembe is responsible for playing accompaniment parts to the rhythm, starting, changing (including calling out special arrangements and variations for the music and the dancers), as well as stopping the music and dance. Typically, this is done by one Djembefola at a time to eliminate confusion unless the ensemble is called to join in. Djembefola's are not alone in the festivities. The actual rhythm of the foundation is provided by the **Dunun/DounDoun** drums. These drums are double-sided with cowhide and are played with sticks. The number of Dununs in any ensemble can vary due to many different reasons, including tradition, artistic choice, and availability of Dununs at the time. Keep in mind that most of African culture universally is family-oriented, so houses in the village, names of drums, and any other facets of village life on the continent will have "family-themed" titles. Of the Malinke that reside outside of present-day Mali typically play with three distinctly pitched Dununs, and they are called: **Songban/Songba** (referred to as the Mother/heartbeat of the rhythm) **Dununba/DounDounba** (referred to as the Papa/ the power of the rhythm) and **Kenkeni** (referred to as the baby/ timekeeper of the rhythm).

These drums come together and make beautiful melodies that will accompany naming ceremonies, weddings, funerary precessions, and so much more. Drum and dance is a mechanism within Mande culture that will allow for the many diverse ethnic groups to share a beautiful tradition that helps define who they are as a meta ethnicity. To understand what part to play and what step to take after the music has begun is to understand Malinke culture. Some extra info about differentiating Djembe communities: 1. Malian Djembe music is traditionally played with five Dununs. They have a certain "funky flavor" about their rhythms as well, not unlike some -school hip hop music like "Sugar Hill Gang" and "Big Daddy Kane". 2. Senegalese Djembes are very heavy and usually on the shorter side. 3. Ivorian Djembes have a smaller head in diameter, and rhythms from the **Guro** are very fast with many complex arrangements. 4. Many performances will start with a 'Drum talk", a conversation had amongst the musicians to come together and vibe so they can play for the dancers. 5. First break is for the music; the second is for the dancers.

Now that we have refreshed ourselves with the basics of the Djembe orchestra, let's test our knowledge of the Malinke traditions:

Questions

1.Djembe music comes from Ancient Egypt and is the oldest music in the world. True or False?

2.The "break" is played by any drum in the Djembe orchestra. True or False?

3.Djembe can be found during what occasions?

4.Who are the Numu?

5.Senegalese Djembes are extremely light and don't weigh very much. True or False?

6.How many drums are in the Djembe orchestra?

7.What is the role of the Djembefola?

8.Where is Djembe music from?

9.Are we connected to the Malinke?

10.How do our Malinke brothers and sisters feel about us? Hint: think back on a video Kofi Piesie Research Team did where we interviewed or Gambain M'boka.

11. Djembe can be found around the world. True or False?

12. Malinke plays djembe after a successful time of fishing down by the river and ocean. What rhythm is played for said celebration?

13. What happens when young men need to settle a rivalry?

14. Do women play drums?

15. What are some musical distinctions amongst populations that play Djembe?

Lesson 6

The Most Important Organ In Your Body Besides The Heart Is The Brain

Baneta Sutton

The most important organ in your body besides the heart is the brain. It is located inside your skull and makes up the central nervous system along with the spinal cord. The nervous system is how the brain is able to control the actions of your body. The brain and spinal cord work together to send information, called signals. These signals are sent to what are called nerves. Nerves enable your body to do what your brain is directing it to do. The peripheral nervous system controls nerves throughout the entire body. This is how you can feel pain when you are hurt. For example, when a person gets burned, they feel the heat. The intense heat penetrates the nerves, which causes you to feel pain. The brain has many functions. The brain controls everything that your body does, voluntary and involuntary. The heart, however, can beat on its own involuntarily without having any signals coming from the brain.

The brain controls everything we do. It controls thinking, our senses, emotions, speaking, and many other very important actions. There are three parts of the brain, the brain cortex, cerebellum, and encephalic trunk. The cerebellum controls balance, movement, and coordination. The encephalic trunk connects the brain to the spinal cord. It controls digestion, breathing, and pumping blood throughout the body. The brain cortex contains neurons that transmit signals to nervous impulses. The left hemisphere of the brain controls the right side of the body, calculating, speech and reasoning. The right hemisphere controls the left side of the body, intuition, music, art, and creativity.

There are four lobes of the brain, occipital, parietal, frontal, and temporal. The frontal lobe is in charge of planning and emotions. The parietal lobe controls the senses. The temporal lobe controls memory and face recognition. The occipital lobe is in charge of processing visual information. Your brain is really powerful. Scientists have not been able to fully understand how memory works, especially when it comes to dreams and some people being able to so-called "see the future, or prophesy." Have you ever dreamt of something that came true?

Protecting the brain is very important. How do we do this, one may ask? You can protect your brain with a helmet when riding a bike, skating, or riding a motorcycle. Exercise will keep the brain healthy. Sleep is also important. The brain has to rest, so get adequate sleep! Eight to ten hours a night should suffice. Working crossword puzzles and solving riddles is another way to exercise your brain. The brain is very important! It controls almost everything in our body. It controls our emotions, analytical skills, pain, creativity, speech, planning, calculating, and senses. Work your brain, so it can continue to work for you!!

Questions:

1). Where is the brain located?

2). What is the nervous system, and what is its function?

3). What are the nerves called that allow us to feel pain?

4). What are the three parts of the brain called?

5). What are the four lobes?

6). What is the job of the frontal lobe?

7). What is the job of the occipital lobe?

8). What does the cerebellum control?

9). What connects the brain to the spinal cord?

10). What are some ways to protect the brain?

Lesson 7

The Common Sense Problem

By Blak Pantha

There is often the notion that we as humans should use our common sense in everyday life for problems and challenges we face. One must ask themselves, what is this common sense that people tell us to use? Common sense is defined as sound, practical judgment concerning everyday matters, or a basic ability to perceive, understand, and judge in a manner that is shared by (i.e. *common to*) nearly all people. We can deduce that common sense is a body of knowledge shared by people that one should know but what happens when the challenge we face is outside of the common sense scope? One would think that a virus, earthquake, archeological dig, and other scientific phenomenon would be outside of the common sense scope. Yet we see in society humans trying to explain the natural world by using common sense. We must deduce that common sense does not trump empirical research and methodology. In many instances, common sense is subjective, making it an inadequate tool for analysis. The limits of common sense should be acknowledged and understood. Science is defined as the intellectual and practical activity encompassing the systematic study of the structure and behavior of the physical and natural world through observation and experiment. Observation and experiment are what we use to produce evidence or what the young people call receipts. Common sense produces no receipts because there is no testing of the data. Without testing, measuring, and experimenting, common sense becomes an opinion or a hypothesis. A simple understanding of this would halt some of our complaints about people not having what we perceive as common sense. We must become more scientifically minded and follow methods and rigor in our everyday lives. We cannot simply common sense our way through life; contrary to popular belief, our experiences are so different depending on demographics and topics that our "common sense" may be so different to the point that it's unrecognizable by others. How ironic that our common sense cannot be as common as the scientific method? The scientific method is something that doesn't change and is pretty much universal. Its results recorded by top scientists of all creeds, colors, and regions. It is by far a better tool for analysis than the common untested sense we rely on. I challenge you, young brilliant Afrikan mind, to get more into science, for the scientist will undoubtedly change the world. Garvey said we must have our own scientist par excellence; will it be you that takes up that charge?

Questions

1). What is common sense?

2). What is science?

3). What did Marcus Garvey say about science?

4). True or False. Common sense is an accurate tool for analysis?

5). True or False. Are Viruses is the scope of common sense?

Lesson 8

The Spear

Kofi Piesie

Spear

A spear is a pole weapon consisting of a shaft, usually of wood, with a pointed head. The head may be simply the sharpened end of the shaft itself, as is the case with fire-hardened spears, or it may be made of a more durable material fastened to the shaft, such as bone, flint, obsidian, iron, steel, or bronze (or other types of stone or metal). Since ancient times, the most common design for hunting or combat spears has incorporated a metal spearhead shaped like a triangle, lozenge, or leaf. The heads of fishing spears usually feature barbs or serrated edges.

Origin

Archaeological evidence found in present-day Germany documents that wooden spears have been used for hunting since at least 400,000 years ago, and a 2012 study from the site of Kathu Pan in South Africa suggests that hominids, possibly Homo heidelbergensis, may have developed the technology of hafted stone-tipped spears in Africa about 500,000 years ago.

However, wood does not preserve well, and Craig Stanford, a primatologist and professor of anthropology at the University of Southern California, has suggested that the discovery of the spear used by chimpanzees means that early humans may have used wooden spears before this.

I know you like huh chimpanzees use spears?

Chimpanzees are capable of making spears to hunt other primates and have been seen using the weapons to kill bushbabies for meat, scientists announced some time ago.

The scientists investigated the Fongoli community of savannah-dwelling chimpanzees(Pan troglodytes verus) in southeastern Senegal. The researchers saw ten different chimps fashioning spear-like tools to forcibly jab at nocturnal primates known as lesser bushbabies(Galago senegalensis), which sleep inside hollow branches or tree trunks during the day. After their attacks, the chimps sniffed or licked their weapons as if to see whether or not they shed blood.

In 2007 a group of researchers began a study of observing chimp behavior. During that time, they recorded 308 spear hunting events, which they noted, was more common for females than males; they accounted for 61 percent of the total.

The researchers suggest this is likely the case because it is more difficult for females to chase down prey. After all, they almost always have offspring clinging to their bodies. To date, the chimps are the only known animal to use a tool as a weapon to hunt a "large" animal, other than humans—chimps in other troops have been seen to use twigs as tools to help collect termites, but scientists do not count that as hunting.

Questions

1). A spear is a pole weapon consisting of what?

2). What kind of material is the spear head made out of?

3). Spear is used for what?

4). Homo heidelbergensis may have developed the technology of hafted stone-tipped spears in Africa about how many years ago?

5). In present-day Germany, Archaeological found what evidence about the spear?

6). Chimpanzees use the spear to do what?

7). Chimpanzees use the spear as a weapon to hunt what?

8). After their attacks, the chimps do what with the spear?

9). Researchers recorded how many hunting events?

10). To date, the chimps are the only known animal to use a spear as a weapon to do what?

Lesson 9

Filibuster

Donielle Leach

Compare this to a lifetime appointment on the Supreme Court, which only needs a majority vote in the Senate...it's a shameful oppressive go to play that must be defeated.

Why Congress must end the filibuster?

As we move toward the runoff senate races in Georgia that will decide control of the Senate, understanding the use of the filibuster and the need to end it is imperative.

What is the filibuster, you ask?

The filibuster is a powerful legislative device in the United States Senate. Senate rules permit a senator or senators to speak for as long as they wish and on any topic they choose, unless "three-fifths of the Senators duly chosen and sworn (usually 60 out of 100 senators) vote to bring debate to a close by invoking cloture under Senate Rule XXII. Even if a filibuster attempt is unsuccessful, the process takes floor time. Defenders call the filibuster "The Soul of the Senate."

Basically, in order for legislation to move from the debate floor to an actual vote, you need 60 out of 100 senators to vote for cloture.

The filibuster is a jim crow era strategy that began here in the USA after emancipation by Southern states to prevent granting equal rights to newly freed slaves. It was most famously used by South Carolina's Strom Thurmond as he spoke for over 24 hours to prevent the Civil Rights Act of 1964 from passing.

So as we look to hold the Biden/Harris administration accountable (and rightfully so) on a specific mandate for Black America justice and equality, ending things like qualified immunity making police officers think just as much about their wallet and 401K as they think about their gun during encounters with Black Americans, making healthcare more accessible and relieving student debt, creating opportunities for small business grants and public school funding in communities of color, we must first get out the vote in Georgia once again and then end all archaic, racist policies such as the Senate FILIBUSTER...

Why do you think a process such as the filibuster is unfair in a Democracy? Does the filibuster encourage bipartisanship (cooperation between both parties), or does it prevent progress, in your opinion? In today's political environment, can we truly hold the Biden administration accountable for failing to adhere to a mandate for a "black agenda" knowing the political games being played in the legislative branch? With a Democratic majority in the House of representatives and a 50/50 split in the Senate with the vice president holding the tie-breaking vote on legislation, the filibuster stands in the way of progress we seek, things like universal healthcare, student debt relief, free community college, criminal justice reform, reparations (possibly) So what should be done about the intentional stalemate?

Questions

1). What is a filibuster?

2). For legislation to move from the debate floor to an actual vote, how many senators to vote is needed?

3). The filibuster is what kind of strategy?

4). Defenders call filibuster what?

5). Strom Thurmond spoke for how many hours to prevent the civil right act of 1964 from passing?

Lesson 10

Code-Switching

Chavis Tp hsb McCray

"Code-switching is the practice of moving back and forth between two languages or between two dialects or registers of the same language at one time. Code-switching occurs far more often in conversation than in writing. It is also called code-mixing and style-shifting. It is studied by linguist to examine when people do it, such as under what circumstances do bilingual speakers switch from one to another, and it is studied by sociologists to determine why people do it such as how it relates to their belonging to a group or the surrounding context of the conversation (casual professional etc.) "Code-switching performs several functions (Zentella, 1985). First, people may use code-switching to hide fluency or memory problems in the second language (but this accounts for about only 10 percent of code switches). Second, code-switching is used to mark switching from Informal situations (using native languages) to formal situations (using the second language). Third, code-switching is used to exert control, especially between parents and children. Fourth, code-switching is used to align speakers with others in specific situations (e.g., defining oneself as a member of an ethnic group). Code-switching also 'functions to announce specific identities, create certain meanings, and facilitate particular interpersonal relationships' (Johnson, 2000, p. 184)." (William B. Gudykunst, Bridging Differences: Effective Intergroup Communication, 4th ed. Sage, 2004)" (Nordquist, R. 2020) In Asar's work mentioned (Imhotep, 2016, chapter 1 pg. 56) and beyond he touches on "Secret and Play languages" of different tribes essentially demonstrating multiple examples of code switching across Africa that verify the various functions quoted above. This suggests code-switching is just a part of African culture. Engrained in the societal psyche employed for a plethora of reasons…." But that doesn't omit more modern dynamics of the concept that Waring addresses in her article, specifically mentioning the switch made by blacks when interacting with whites. In her article titled "What Is Code-Switching and Why Do Black Americans Do It?" She assesses benefit and consequence of the linguistic phenomenon via testimony of blacks themselves expressing their responses ranging from interviewees bragging about their ability to code-switch: "To some people, I'll say 'He was handsome!' versus 'He fine as hell, girl!' And I think I'm the baddest because I can talk to this group and that group in the same way that they talk." to

"One participant in my study told me that he is perpetually self-conscious about code-switching out of fear that someone would witness his behavior and question his authenticity." (Waring, C. 2018) If we prod this dynamic with our sociological curiosity, we find ourselves asking what was the interviewee benefiting from and why did the other feel self-conscious about their behavior. What is going on here? I think now is the perfect time to introduce. ACCULTURATION in to the assessment and refer back to Dr. Wilson and Vic Webb publication where insight is given to offer psychological and sociolinguistic perspective necessary to see how acculturation plays a role. Webb defines sociolinguistic as "the study of language is in relation to society" expounding further "the study of society-its structured belief, traditions, and practices belong to the discipline of sociology, and sociolinguistics is thus a hybrid discipline which combines sociological and linguistic concepts and techniques to study the role of function of language society." (Webb. V, Sure. Pg.92, 2000). Wilson utilizes this approach in chapter 7 pg. 177 breaking down the sociocultural basis of language behavior stating " it is obvious to even the most casual observer that different races and nationalities speak differently that within races and nations, language and dialect differ according to region, cultural class and educational backgrounds. Yet as we have documented in the foregoing section, no one is born speaking or born with a special predisposition to speak exclusively one particular language or only in his "mother tongue". For apparent adaptive reasons, than human neonate is born with the capacity for learning to speak any language it is exposed to for a certain period of time; consequently, regardless of race, the infant is capable of learning with equal ease any language he is exposed to for the first 94 to 5 years of life" (Wilson, A. 2014) The language relevant to our discussion that Blacks in America learn is English. An article significant to our discussion defines Acculturation as "a process through which a person or group from one culture comes to adopt the practices and values of another culture, while still retaining their own distinct culture. This process is most commonly discussed regarding a minority culture adopting elements of the majority culture, as is typically the case with immigrant groups that are culturally or ethnically distinct from the majority in the place to which they have immigrated." (Cole, N. 2020). The so-called "immigrant" here is the African American. Blacks are the minority forced to accept the English language striped of their native languages forced to assimilate. Kole clarifies the difference stating "Acculturation is not the same as the process of assimilation, though some people use the words interchangeably. Assimilation can be an eventual outcome of the acculturation process, but the process can have other outcomes as well, including rejection, integration, marginalization, and transmutation." (Cole, N. 2020). English was assimilated into the African mind via slavery in case you have been under a rock the past 400 years and was not aware. On pg 178, Wilson gives a brief history of the black dialect, which we could argue equates to AAVE, describing " black American dialects are probably the result of creolized form of English, at one time spoken on the southern plantations by black slaves. This creolized plantation English appears to be related to the creolized English spoken by some blacks in Jamaica other Caribbean Islands. Through the interaction with white speech, the black dialect can no longer be considered true Creole dialects, but still, they maintain many Creole features structural characteristics. Africans who were captured as slaves and brought to the New World were forced to learn to use some type of English" (Wilson, A. 2014). In an article titled "The Limits of Standard English" explains AAVE as " a dialect no less complex or expressive than more prestigious forms of the language. It is rule-bound and systematic.

Questions

1). What is code-switching?

2). Does code-switching happen more through writing or speaking?

3). What are other terms for code-switching?

4). Why is code-switching studied linguist?

5). Why do sociologists study code-switching?

6). Who touches on secret and play languages?

7). What account for 10 percent of code switches?

8). Do people mark switching from native languages to second language?

9). How do parents and children use code-switching?

10). What type of situation would code switching be used to align speakers with others?

11). Sociolinguistics is defined as the study of language in relation to what?

12). A process through which a person or group from one culture comes to adopt the practices and values of another culture while still retaining their own distinct culture is known as what?

13). Is acculturation the same as assimilation?

14). Does Black English or black dialect equate to African American Vernacular English?

15). Can assimilation be an eventual outcome of acculturation?

Lesson 11

Comprehensive Finance

Setepenre Meri Amen

Finance and commerce, the exchange of goods and services these concepts have been around for thousands of years. Once value is assigned, demand is created back in the day; there was this thing called a bartering system, which is a method of exchange without the presence of fiat. Nowadays, we use the fiat currency system, ever since 1971 when Nixon to the US dollar off the gold standard. In doing that, the US seen a spike in inflation where interest rates rose over 20 percent yikes! The only people who do well when interest rates are high are those who have fixed-rate debt. Other methods of edging inflation are investing in gold and bonds.

The stock market is publicly traded companies that issue shares of their company to essentially raise money from the public to conduct various business endeavors. There are three major indices that companies are weighted on to measure how the market is doing; those are The S&P 500, The Dow Jones Industrial Average, and the Nasdaq Composite. In 1993 the first ETF "exchange-traded fund," was created ticker symbol SPY. Etf's where created to give investors more exposure to the market in one particular security. In my opinion, ETF's are a safe way to enter the market and see returns year over year.

Bitcoin and Ethereum are the new forms of currency called Cryptocurrency; these two are the top two by market cap. Some say the founder of Bitcoin is Satoshi Nakamoto, but no one really knows. These are digital currency created for peer-to-peer exchange, cutting out the middlemen aka the central banking system. Hence the word "DeFi" which means decentralized finance that trades on the blockchain of Bitcoin or Ethereum.

Questions

1).What are the three major indices in the United States?

2). What is a stock?

3). What is an EFT?

4). What are bonds?

5). What are derivatives in finance?

6). What is cryptocurrency?

7). What is Bitcoin?

8). Who is the said founder of Bitcoin?

9). What is DeFi?

10). What is a Blockchain?

11). How many companies are weighted in the Dow Jones Industrial Average?

12). In what year was the New York Stock Exchange formed?

13). What are the top two cryptocurrencies by market cap?

14). What year did the United States leave the gold standard?

15). What is the best hedge against inflation?

Lesson 12

Who Stole You?
By: Ini-Herit Shawn P

Several hundred years ago, a group of 10 individuals was fishing off the River Niger. Each of them had been successful this day, and as they gathered their things to head back home, a group of strangers approached them with what looked like weapons. Along with their fish, these individuals had been escorted to a canoe close by and then a caravel ship that would set sail to a place far from what these ten individuals knew as home. These ten individuals were of Edo ethnic group located in Southern Nigeria known for their dress and beads. However, none of that meant anything to the people who had just kidnapped these individuals. These individuals were now captives, and what the future held for them, no one could ever imagine. After 12 moon rises and sunsets, the Caravel docked right off the shores of Lisbon. These Edo men shackled, and sweaty far from home stripped of their clothing, identity, and culture suddenly became the property of a people in the blink of an eye. Their language barrier did not matter, beliefs did not matter, human rights did not matter. The only thing that mattered was the fact that they had become the property of a people who neither of them could communicate with nor ever understand—forced into hard labor, caged like an animal, and disrespected beyond human belief. Back home among the Edo people, they had no idea what happened to the ten individuals who sat out to go fishing. Stories began to travel among the people, and some would assume a rival tribe had captured them. Other tales mentioned that the River God was not pleased and had claimed their lives. Another story said a strange bird that flew in off the coastline carrying pale skin, overly dressed people who unwrapped a canoe and took to the Niger with weapons and came back with what possibly could have been the missing Edo people. This story was told by children whose elders initially shunned the idea of such a thing happening. Still, traces of evidence began to reveal themselves, leading numerous people to the shoreline to find evidence that substantiated the children's story. As the town gathered to address the potential threat of foreign entities kidnapping people, they began to devise plans that would help them counter the next potential danger; however, no one could predict the next time these strangers would appear; however, this troubling alarm meant that a people would one day potentially be under-siege.

Questions

1). How many people went fishing along the Niger River?

2). Where are the kidnapped victims from?

3). What is the name of the ethnic group associated with the kidnapped victims?

4). True or False: The Edo are known for having a lot of gold?

5). Are the Edo located in Cameroon?

6). How many times did the moon rise before the victims reached land?

7). What kind of ship did the Edo board?

8). Did the Caravel travel the River Niger?

9). Is it true that the Edo knew what happened to the ten individuals that had not returned?

10). Did the Edo find evidence of the kidnapped leading them from the River Niger to the Atlantic?

Lesson 13

The Use Of IT For AfrakaN Development

Tanehesi The Restorer's

I've always wanted to write a book that focuses on the development of young minds that would be skilled in the application and use of IT (information technology) for modern development. Recently, the opportunity surfaces when wise arakunrin Kofi asked me to contribute to such a book. So I suggested that I could contribute to this project by providing a chapter that focuses on the development of young minds to understand the scientific application of IT in modern-day scenarios. In this age which is shaped primarily by information and technology, it is important for young minds to escape the traps of miseducation and religion and adapt the fundamentals of the Modern Scientific approach.

What Challenges?

Of course, there will be challenges, but such things are only obstacles that methodology and perspective will allow us to escape. For example, teaching the youth about App and web development not only enhances their critical thinking and problem-solving skills but it also enhances their ingenuity and empowers them to address the various challenges of development. The skills required also can supply the youth with an opportunity for mobility with jobs and projects surfacing anywhere around the world and especially AfRaKa. A good example of this potential is the need for the development of apps in the areas of Education, Medicine and Health, E-commerce, and other sectors. For young minds to accept this challenge is for the betterment of their communities and their families.

Like Tanzania, AfRaKa needs technology centers where application and other tools can be studied and produced by young AfRaKaN Scientific thinkers who also understand the existential need to preserve their traditional AfRaKan cultural perspectives. In this regard, teaching AfRaKaN centered IT perspectives will allow them to escape their concepts and ideas regarding AfRaKaN development. Not only can apps be developed for non-commercial reasons but also for commercial reasons, which could translate into sources of income for the youth and their families and communities.

Questions

1). How to nourish critical thinking skills and to identify the youth with IT potential?

2). How to safeguard the preservation of traditional sense of identity and culture along with the integration of IT?

3). Do we understand the difference between Web and Application Development?

4). Teaching the youth how to copyright and protect their intellectual property and creations?

5). How to Register and Build a Web Site?

6). Teaching the youth how to build and publish apps for Android devices?

7). Teaching the youth how to build and publish apps for App devices?

8). How to write a Business Plan?

9). How to source funding or get a Bank loan?

10). Best countries for IT?

Lesson 14

How to Make Herb-Infused Oils for Culinary & Body Care Use

Sophia Catching

Making Herbal -Infused oils

OIL INFUSING BASICS:

While most herbs can be infused either dried or fresh (with proper preparation), some lend themselves better to one form than the other. A famous example is St. John's wort, which is widely believed to require fresh material to create an effective herbal oil.

Herbal oils can turn rancid or grow mold, especially if the carrier oil used is not very shelf-stable (such as rosehip seed oil) or if fresh herbs are used. Infused oils that exhibit any change in color, scent, clarity, or taste should be discarded for safety. Using the alcohol intermediary infusion method or adding a preservative like vitamin E can help keep oils stable longer, but it will also make them unsuitable for eating.

Herbs with natural dyes may be infused in oil for use in adding color to soaps and other body care formulations.

You may want to wear gloves when it comes time to strain a finished herbal oil through a cheesecloth-lined strainer and to squeeze out any oil remaining in the herbs. While you can use your bare hands, working with oils is a messy process, and certain herbs, like turmeric, may temporarily stain your hands and jewelry.

Often, the oil will not wash out of cheesecloth or muslin, so make sure you strain with something you're not going to reuse.

Even after straining, fine herb sediment can make oil a bit gritty—if this bothers you, strain again through a coffee filter. This is a slow-drip process and may require more than one coffee filter to strain all the oil.

You can blend herbs together for synergistic infusions. For example, hops flowers, lavender flowers, and chamomile flowers infused together in jojoba oil make a wonderful relaxing blend for use with massage. Mix and match to suit your needs!

Questions

1). What should you wear when infusing oils because they can be messy?

2). Name an item you can use to strain your infusion?

3). Name a carrier oil that can be used for a relaxing massage?

4). When straining oil, can you use a coffee liner?

5). Is it possible for your infusion to be gritty if not thoroughly strained?

6). Name the process used to strain herbs when using a coffee filter?

7). Can You use Coloring to your infusions?

8). Can Infusions go rancid or Mold?

9). What oil can be used to keep infusions from going bad?

10). Name a popular infusion that uses fresh herbs?

11). Besides Vitamin E, what else can be used to preserve your infusion?

12). Name a herb that can stain your Hands and or jewelry?

13). What other creations can herbs be used in?

14). Can Fresh, or Dried Herbs Be used for Infusions?

15). Name 3 flowers that can be used for synergistic infusions?

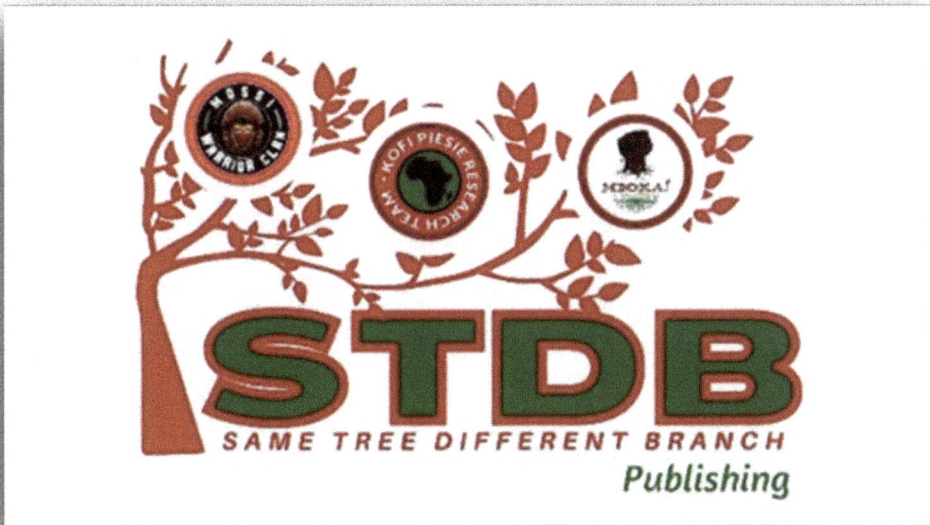

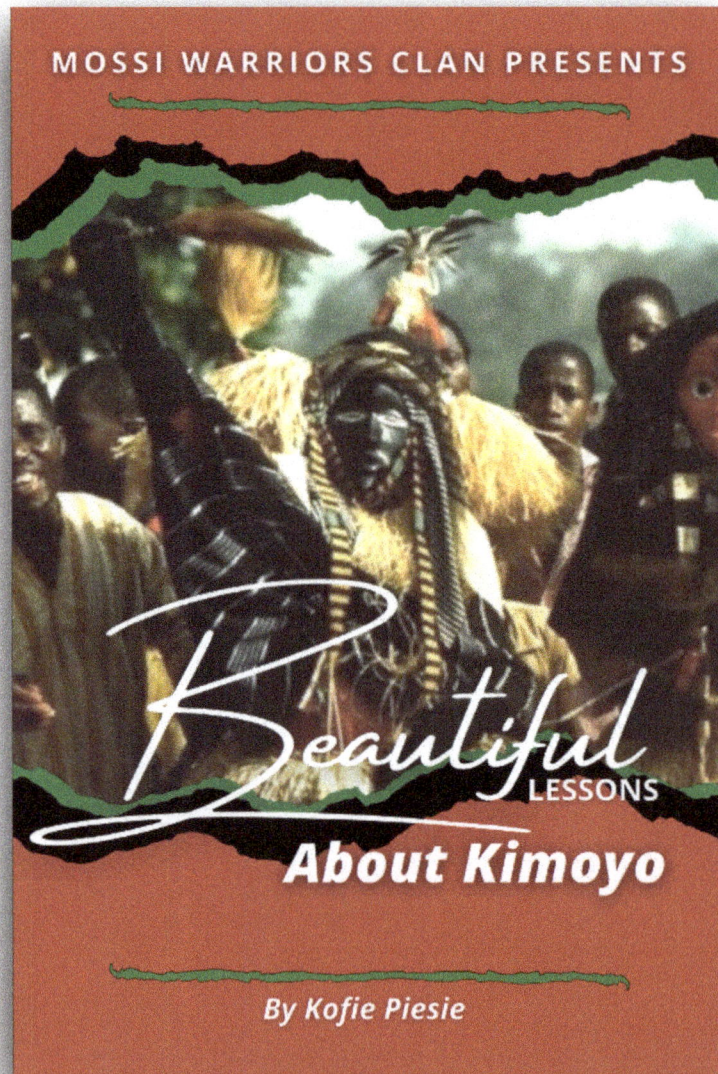

MOSSI WARRIORS CLAN PRESENTS

Beautiful LESSONS
About Kimoyo

By Kofie Piesie

MOSSI WARRIOR CLAN PRESENT

DINKA
APPROVED

SPEAR MASTERS

A Historical Survey of the Minds of
African Warrior Scholars Vol. 4

By Kofi Tesie Research Team

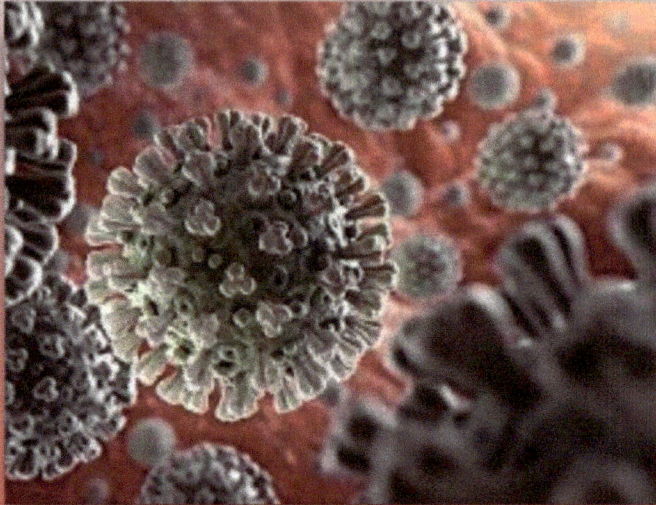

MOSSI WARRIOR CLAN PRESENT

What Sars-CoV2 Taught Me

By: Ini-Herit Shawn P

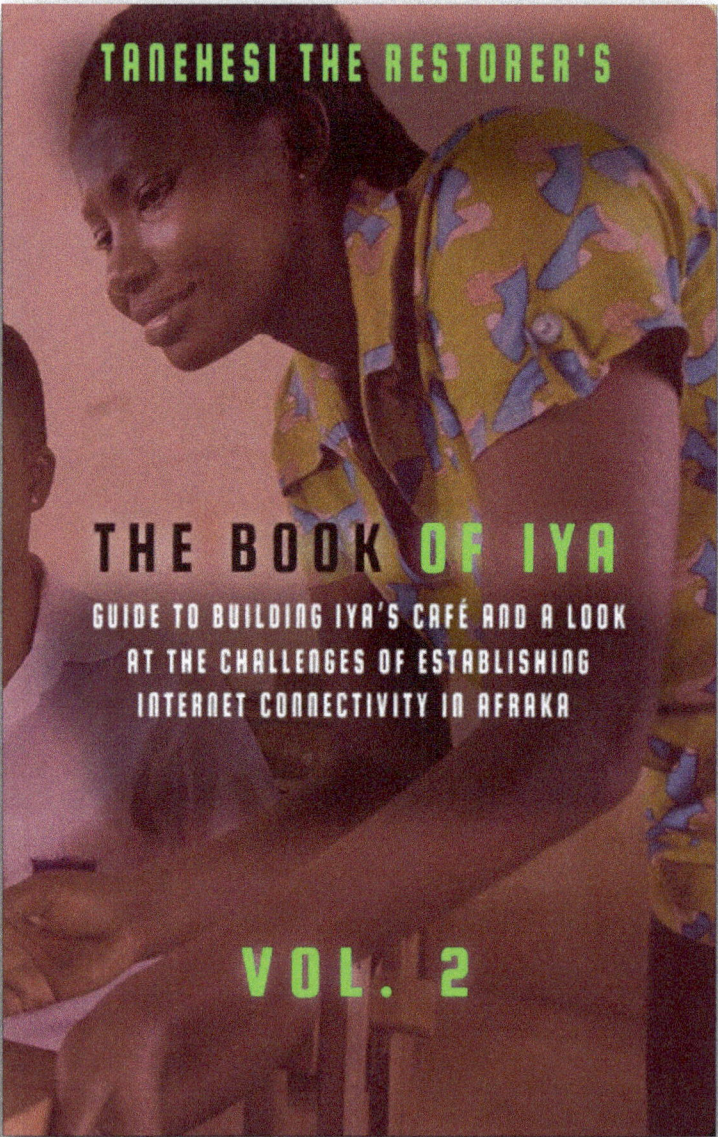

TANEHESI THE RESTORER'S

THE BOOK OF IYA

GUIDE TO BUILDING IYA'S CAFÉ AND A LOOK AT THE CHALLENGES OF ESTABLISHING INTERNET CONNECTIVITY IN AFRAKA

VOL. 2

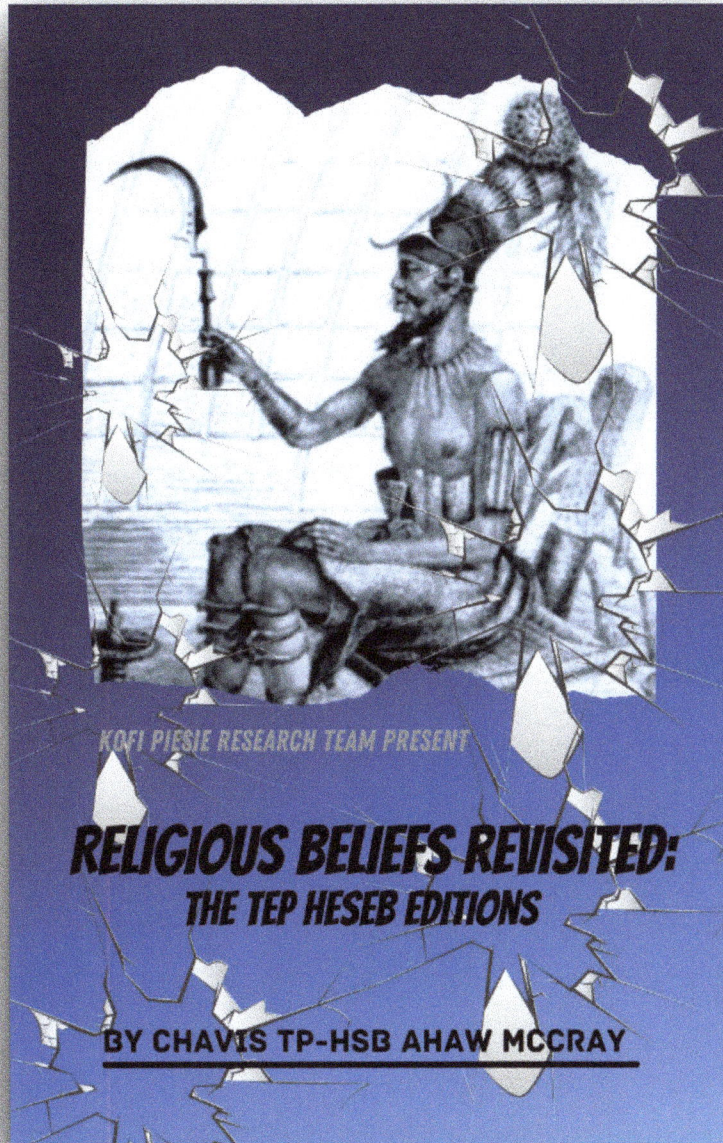

KOFI PIESIE RESEARCH TEAM PRESENT

RELIGIOUS BELIEFS REVISITED:
THE TEP HESEB EDITIONS

BY CHAVIS TP-HSB AHAW MCCRAY

SPEAR MASTERS INSTITUTION
COLORING BOOK 1

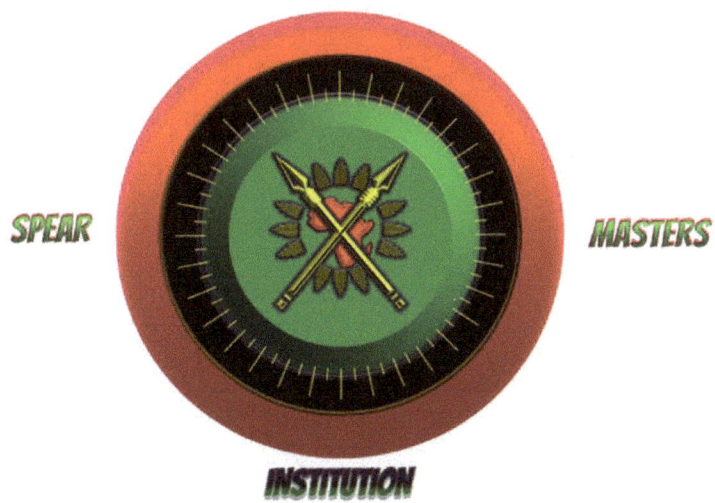

SPEAR MASTERS INSTITUTION

www.ingramcontent.com/pod-product-compliance
Lightning Source LLC
Chambersburg PA
CBHW061412090426

42741CB00023B/3490